THE
INNOVATION
IMPERATIVE

How Extraordinary Leaders
Sustain the Spark

Vanya Boardman
Austin Roberts

ISBN: 978-1-970962-00-0 (Paperback)
ISBN: 978-1-970962-01-7 (Hardcover)
ISBN: 978-1-970962-02-4 (Ebook)

LCCN: 2025926074

First edition

Published by PlayInnové LLC
Sacramento, California, USA
www.playinnove.com

Disclaimer:
This book is for educational and informational purposes only. The authors and publisher are not responsible for any actions taken based on the content of this book.

Contents

For those who choose curiosity over certainty,
connection over competition,
and courage over comfort.

INTRODUCTION:

Ever Wonder: Why Would Anyone Want to Work Here?

The future of work isn't just remote or hybrid or AI-enabled. It's deeply human. And deeply in need of reinvention.

THE TO-DO LIST is endless. The inbox never empties. You keep hearing words like innovation, engagement, and resilience, as if you can just summon them out of thin air.

You care deeply about the people you work with, but most days, you're running on fumes yourself. You're tired, overwhelmed, stretched too thin, and still expected to lead innovation, engagement, and magic.

You're not alone. Across industries and hierarchies, leaders everywhere are quietly asking the same question:

How did work become so hard to feel good about?

According to Gallup, only about 21% of employees worldwide feel truly engaged at work.

That means nearly four out of five people are simply going through the motions, exhausted, disconnected, and searching for meaning in the hours that fill most of their lives. And when people lose meaning, culture drifts, innovation stalls, and burnout spreads.

We've seen it too, in startups, hospitals, tech companies,

and global giants alike. Talented people showing up, but not lighting up.

The truth is, most teams aren't broken. They just get lost in competing priorities.

Too busy to pause, to breathe, to see each other. Too focused on outputs to align with their purpose. Too drained to play, which means too tired to imagine what's possible. And yet, that's the very rhythm that makes work better.

Pause sharpens our presence. Purpose gives our work meaning. Play brings energy and learning through experience.

Because when we play, we don't just relax, we learn by doing. We test, explore, and discover together. Play transforms theory into experience and experience into wisdom.

Together, these three elements—Pause, Purpose, and Play, form a loop, a human operating system for creativity and connection.

When one fades, culture drifts. When all three align, culture hums.

So the question isn't "How do we keep people engaged?" It's "How do we help them pause, find purpose, and rediscover the joy of work through playful shared experience?"

Oh No, Not Another Culture Book

Let's be honest, there's no shortage of books about workplace culture.

Books to lead better, to communicate clear, to motivate teams and shift into gear. Frameworks, models, checklists galore, acronyms stacked and still leaving us wanting more. Some pages truly inspire, but few deliver the wisdom stream.

"So... how exactly do I use this with my team?"

That's the question that started this book.

It was born from the real, messy, hopeful work of sitting with teams, listening, experimenting, laughing, and sometimes failing right alongside them.

From boardrooms to break rooms, we've watched people come alive again. Not because they were told what to do, but because they were invited to connect, reflect, and imagine. To pause with presence, act with purpose, and re-energize through playful experience.

Because culture isn't a policy, it's a pulse. It's the feeling people get when they walk into work.

Do they feel seen? Heard? Safe to speak up? Trusted to try something new?

That's what this book explores, the micro-moments, rituals, and choices that turn workplaces into communities, and teams into catalysts for change.

The Power of Pause, Purpose, and Play

Each part of this book invites you to build a new habit for how work can feel.

Part One - Pause: How presence and reflection reset our pace and open space for better thinking.

Part Two - Purpose: How connection, gratitude, and meaning turn work into contribution.

Part Three - Play: How creativity and experience transform energy into innovation.

Pause gives clarity. Purpose gives direction. Play gives energy, and the experience that helps lessons stick.

Together, they help teams not just perform, but come alive again.

A Personal Invitation

From scrappy startups to global enterprises, we've seen one truth repeat.

Even great teams can lose their spark, but they can get it back too.

When we pause with presence, act with purpose, and engage through play, we reawaken what work was meant to be: human, connected, alive.

So if you're ready to pause with purpose and play with intention, not to escape the work, but to transform it, let's begin.

CHAPTER 1:

Presence with Purpose

"Attention is the rarest and purest form of generosity."

— Simone Weil

Show Up Before You Speak Up

BEFORE A TEAM can collaborate, innovate, or grow, they must first **arrive**. Not just log in. Not just sit down. But be *present*. Fully. Intentionally. Wholeheartedly.

Presence is the unspoken agreement we make with one another:

"I am here with you. My head isn't buried in my inbox. My mind isn't replaying yesterday's mistakes or jumping to tomorrow's to-do list. I'm here."

At PlayInnové, we've seen it again and again: Teams that learn how to be present achieve everything else faster: trust, innovation, focus, and flow. A Harvard study on mindfulness at work showed that even brief presence practices improve focus and reduce stress by up to 30%. Plus, pause strengthens decision-making. Both advantages compound into better performance and faster outcomes.

The Lost Art of Arrival

Most meetings begin in motion. Someone's rushing in late. Someone else is distracted, still halfway in another task. Laptops open. Notifications ping. Technically, everyone's in the room… but no one is really there.

A few intentional seconds can shift everything! That's what sprinters do in the blocks. What jazz musicians do before the downbeat. What teachers do when they close the door and breathe in before class begins.

Great moments don't start with movement. They start with presence. They start with *pause*.

Why *Pause* Works

History shows us that great leaders, artists, and thinkers have always leaned on *pause* to find clarity and connection.

- Aristotle's students earned the nickname *Peripatetics* - "those who walk about," because he taught while strolling in the gardens.
- Beethoven carried sketchbooks on hikes, capturing melodies that emerged from the stillness of nature.
- Steve Jobs made walking meetings a habit, a practice Tim Cook and other CEOs still carry on.
- Winston Churchill, under wartime pressure, found grounding in painting and reflective walks on his estate.
- And even more recently, Mary Barra, CEO of General Motors, *pauses* to walk the floors and listen. In those quiet moments, clarity replaces noise.

Across centuries, the pattern is clear: *pause* isn't wasted time. It's fertile ground where clarity, creativity, and courage take root. Modern neuroscience affirms this: intentional presence activates brain networks tied to creativity, while even short pauses reduce stress hormones and improve memory.

Pause isn't passive. It's a performance enhancer.

It isn't only history and science, it's also supported by modern leadership research. One of our mentors, Dr. Steven Ralph, studied *pause* practices in his work, *Exploring the Relationship Between Creativity Training and the Practice of Pause for Leaders in a World of Information Overload* (2017). His findings echo what both science and history suggest: *pause* practices increase engagement, reduce overload, deepen creativity, and transform leadership training experiences.

Pause is not an interruption to leadership. It is leadership.

If *pause* has been the secret of philosophers, composers, statesmen, and CEOs, the question for us becomes: how can we practice it in our day to day? How can leaders and teams design moments that shift us from distraction to presence, from noise to clarity? Presence with purpose is not about slowing down for its own sake. It's about choosing *pauses* that sharpen focus, deepen connection, and prepare us for what matters most.

What might happen if our teams began to see *pause* not as wasted time but as a strategic tool? Presence with purpose begins when we stop asking, *"Do we have time to pause?"* and start asking, *"Can we afford not to?"* Because presence with purpose is what turns *pause* into progress.

From Theory to Practice

Principle:

Be here now, fully and with intention.

Practice:

Take one minute at the start of a meeting for a collective *pause*. Begin with a Pulse Check or Arrival Breath.

- *"In one word, how are you arriving today?"*
- *"What's something you're leaving at the door so you can be present here?"*
- *"Let's take one deep breath together before we begin."*

This isn't fluff; it's **focus strategy.**

Playful Ritual:

The Moment of *Pause*

Establish meeting openers that create transitions from hustle to presence. Use music, a quote, an image, or even build with LEGO® bricks to ground the group in the now.

Example Prompts:

- If your current mindset were a song or famous quote, what would it be?
- If you could bring one unexpected guest into this meeting; a historical figure, a fictional character, even a superhero, who would it be and why? (for virtual meetings: be prepared to share an image of your character)
- Using LEGO® Bricks, take 2 minutes to create a model of something small you're grateful for right now.

Over time, these rituals don't just settle the room; they shape culture. They remind people that presence is the priority.

Application in Action

We worked with a global facilities team that shared they were struggling with tension and disconnection. Meetings often felt heavy, communication frequently broke down, team members were reluctant to take on new projects, and support for one another was lacking.

To create space for connection, we introduced a new standard: **no meeting begins without a presence *pause*.** Using Gloria Willcox's Feelings Wheel as a guide:

Each person was invited to identify one word that captured how they were able to show up in the meeting. We paired this with three additional questions:

- Is there anything distracting you from being fully present that the team should be aware of?
- Do you need any specific support today?
- Is there something specific you want to be sure we cover in this discussion?

At first, the practice felt silly and quite awkward. The team bonded over jokes about the feelings wheel. But over time and with repetition, those moments became the most important part of the meeting. The team grew more comfortable sharing what they were experiencing, where they needed support, and what mattered most, both professionally and personally. Over time, they even began asking, "Where's the wheel?" if it wasn't on the screen at the start of each meeting.

With repetition, the presence *pause* shifted the team culture. Meetings became more cohesive, supportive, collaborative and more effective, even across multiple time zones and facilities. What began as a simple ritual to check-in, transformed into a habit of personal connection that elevated team trust and performance.

Supporting Models & Theories

- **Cognitive Load Theory (Sweller):** Pausing improves information retention and executive function
- **Emotional Contagion Theory:** Leaders who model calm and focused presence shape the mood of the room
- **FLOW State Theory (Csikszentmihalyi):** Presence is a prerequisite for deep work and peak creativity
- **Mindful Leadership (Harvard Business Review):** Conscious attention improves decision-making and team morale

Reflect + Try This

- **Self-Check:** *Pause*, and ask...
- *"What might I need to set down to really arrive here?"*
- *"Am I arriving with intention, and what is that intention?"*
- *"If presence is generosity, what am I giving right now?"*

- **Team Practice:** Start the next team check-in with a one-word mood check. Reflect at the end of the meeting: *"Did that small pause make a difference?"*
- **Leader Action:** Choose just one meeting per week to open with stillness, not slides. (Think James Clear's Atomic Habits, "1% better.")

Closing Thought

Presence is the beginning of every meaningful moment. It's how we build trust. It's how we avoid costly mistakes. It's how we honor the people and ideas in front of us.

To be present is to say: *"This matters. You matter. Let's build something worth showing up for, together."*

CHAPTER 2:

Listen Generously

"Most people do not listen with the intent to understand; they listen with the intent to reply."
— *Stephen Covey*

The Quiet Superpower

IN A WORLD wired for speed, speaking up gets celebrated while listening, the quieter partner in communication, is too often neglected. Yet, if you ask anyone to describe a truly transformative conversation, it almost always includes the feeling of being deeply heard.

Generous listening isn't just about letting someone talk, it's about creating **space**. Space for people to reveal what they really think. Space to change course. Space to belong.

At PlayInnové, we've found that **generous listening is a gateway to psychological safety** (as a reminder, psychological safety is a shared belief that it's safe to speak up, take risks, and make mistakes without fear of punishment or humiliation). When a teammate truly feels heard, they feel safe to experiment, speak up, and show up. In that safety, innovation takes root.

A Brief History of Listening

Many Indigenous cultures have long practiced **talking or listening circles**. In these spaces, listening is sacred: no interruptions, no arguments, only the trust that each voice will be heard.

In **Buddhist Sanghas**, listening is part of mindfulness itself: to sit with another's words without judgment, to hear with compassion rather than rebuttal. This practice has shaped spiritual communities across Asia for centuries.

In **Japan**, the tradition of **nemawashi** emphasizes listening before deciding. Leaders and stakeholders engage in quiet, informal conversations to understand perspectives, build trust, and surface concerns long before proposals are finalized. It is leadership by listening first, acting second.

In the United States, **Abraham Lincoln**, even amid the Civil War, was known for listening with patience and respect. He sought out voices often ignored, such as Black soldiers, political opponents, and dissenting cabinet members. He believed that true leadership meant hearing every perspective before making decisions.

Later, in 1933, **Franklin D. Roosevelt** began his famous Fireside Chats. While the world reeled from economic collapse, he chose not a podium but a radio microphone. His tone was conversational, even warm, because he had spent the week listening to advisors, letters, and the public mood before he spoke. Americans felt heard, even through the static of radio.

Across cultures and centuries, the message is the same: listening is not passive. It is the foundation of belonging, trust, and transformation.

Why It Matters in the Workplace

Modern teams often confuse "debate" with "dialogue."

- In debate, people try to win.
- In dialogue, people try to understand.

That difference changes everything. Research from Harvard Business Review and MIT's Human Dynamics Lab found that high-performing teams share a striking trait: *equal airtime and active listening.* These teams don't just talk more; they listen more, especially to quieter voices.

Other studies echo this:

- **Google's Project Aristotle** identified psychological safety as the single most important factor in team success.

- **McKinsey's research on inclusion** shows that when leaders actively listen to underrepresented voices, organizations see measurable gains in engagement, retention, and innovation.

- **Neuroscience studies** suggest that when people feel genuinely listened to, stress hormones decrease, oxytocin (the bonding chemical) increases, and the prefrontal cortex, the part of the brain tied to problem-solving and empathy, becomes more active.

Generous listening reduces defensiveness, strengthens trust, and creates the kind of creative tension that fuels bold new ideas. In other words, it doesn't just make people feel good, it makes teams perform better.

From Theory to Practice

Principle:

Hear beyond words and create space for others.

Practice:
Use "Listen + Reflect" Rounds

In your next meeting, introduce a round where each person shares a thought or update. The next person must first reflect back what they heard and then add their own thought. This creates a chain of attentiveness. No one is rehearsing their reply. Everyone is listening to understand.

Playful Ritual:
One Voice at a Time

Designate certain segments of meetings as "listening zones." No cross-talk, no interruptions, just presence. Create space for voices that don't usually get the floor.

Examples:

- Use a simple object (like a stress ball, stuffed animal, or even a fidget stick). Only the person holding it speaks; everyone else practices intentional listening.

- Use a virtual or physical spinner with names. Whoever it lands on speaks next, ensuring everyone gets a turn.

- Quiet brainstorming: everyone writes their thoughts on a sticky note, then one by one the notes are read aloud without debate or identification. We're just listening first.

Application in Action:

During one of our LEGO® SERIOUS PLAY® workshops, a remote employee, known for being reliable but rarely vocal in meetings, was invited to build and share her model surrounding better team communication. The process gave her the floor in a way that couldn't be sidestepped or overshadowed.

When she spoke, she surprised her colleagues and leadership with a powerful insight: the team needed dedicated "get to know you" sessions for remote staff, complete with simple, playful activities to strengthen connection across distance. Her suggestions were so thoughtful and immediately practical that several were implemented right away.

The CEO later reflected that while the remote employee had always excelled in her sales role, this moment revealed untapped potential. What shifted wasn't just her confidence, it was the team's willingness to listen generously.

This is the heart of generous listening: it uncovers brilliance in places we often overlook. When we design structures that create space for every voice, especially the quiet ones, we don't just hear more, we become more, as a team.

Supporting Models & Theories

- **Carl Rogers' Active Listening:** The foundation of empathy-based dialogue
- **Amy Edmondson's Psychological Safety:** Listening as a trust-building behavior
- **The Trust Triangle (HBR):** "Empathy" as one of the three pillars, best expressed through listening

Reflect + Try This

- **Self-Check:** "Am I listening to connect, or just to reply?" "Am I listening to understand?"
- **Team Practice:** During your next brainstorm, try a "No Response" rule for 10 minutes. Let each idea land, with no judgment or additions.
- **Leader Action:** Ask, *"Whose voice haven't we heard?"* at least once per meeting.

Closing Thought

Listening generously isn't just a team skill. It's a cultural reset. It says: "You belong here. Your ideas matter. I'm not just waiting for my turn, I'm here for *you*." And in a world full of noise, that's the clearest signal of all.

CHAPTER 3:

Assume Positive Intent

"Assuming good intent is the first step toward building trust."

— *Indra Nooyi*

A Small Gesture, a Big Assumption

During the Cuban Missile Crisis, U.S. officials received two letters from Soviet leader Nikita Khrushchev: one conciliatory and one aggressive. President John F. Kennedy's team faced a choice: which letter reflected Khrushchev's true intent?

Kennedy chose to respond to the conciliatory one, assuming goodwill instead of hostility. Historians suggest that this decision helped de-escalate the standoff and avoid nuclear war.

It was a powerful reminder: how we interpret intent can change the course of history.

The Trust Default

Imagine this: You're in a meeting. Someone rolls their eyes as you speak. Your brain does a backflip: *They hate my idea. They don't respect me. They're just difficult.* But what if their contact lens slipped?

We are **hardwired to fill in gaps** and often, we do it with fear, not faith. **Assuming positive intent** doesn't mean ignoring red flags or excusing harm. It means making a choice. A choice **to interpret others through a lens of curiosity, not criticism.** To leave space for missteps, growth, and grace.

We've seen firsthand how this single principle changes the tone of a team. It's the quiet hero of healthy culture. When people believe they won't be blamed, they bring more. When they're trusted, they take more ownership. When they're met with understanding, they're more willing to stretch and fail forward.

A Moment from Mandela

When Nelson Mandela walked free after 27 years in prison, he chose to sit down with those who had locked him up.

Why?

Because his mission wasn't *revenge;* it was *reconciliation.* Mandela believed most people, even those who had wronged him, were products of a broken system. His default was: *understand the system, assume the human.*

This was not naïveté. It was leadership rooted in trust. Not because people had earned it, but because trust is what transforms them.

Teams That Assume the Best... Do Better

When leaders assume positive intent, it has a **measurable ripple effect.** Studies show that teams led with trust experience:

- **23% greater energy levels**
- **76% more engagement**
- **50% higher productivity**

One growing company we worked with had a major siloing problem. Marketing thought product was being secretive. Product thought marketing didn't listen. The solution wasn't more meetings, it was a shared agreement: *assume good intentions, ask good questions.*

The following quarter, project delays dropped, feedback improved, and people started saying things like, *"I don't feel as on edge anymore."*

That's culture change!

From Theory to Practice

Principle:

Start with trust, especially in challenge.

Practice:

Reframe conflict by asking, "What else might be true?"
Instead of jumping to judgment, slow down and zoom out.
Reflect on other reasons a behavior might be showing up.

Prompt:

"What's the kindest possible explanation for this?"

Playful Ritual:

Curiosity Circles

When tension builds, pause for a facilitated modeling conversation. Each person uses LEGO® bricks to model their intention. Others reflect back what they heard, not what they assume. No solutions just clarification and connection through systems play.

Application in Action

A colleague of ours, who is also a young leader, recently hired a new assistant. Within a month, she noticed some of her meeting invites carried the shorthand "f/u," for example, a meeting titled "f/u Dr. Smith." To our friend's eyes, though, every calendar entry looked like it was shouting something else entirely: "FU."

Her first reaction was discomfort. Could this be intentional? What does this mean? Instead of assuming the worst, though, she paused, got curious, and asked about it kindly and with a little humor. The assistant explained that "f/u" simply meant "follow-up."

What could have been an awkward or even trust-eroding misunderstanding turned into a team inside joke. They laughed about it together, and the shorthand became commonplace in the office. It also became a running source of humor rather than tension.

By choosing to assume positive intent, this young leader not only avoided unnecessary conflict but also built a bridge of connection and trust. Sometimes the best culture-builders are found in small, human missteps handled with grace.

Supporting Models & Theories

- **HBR Trust Triangle:** Positive intent builds empathy, the foundation of trust
- **Attribution Theory:** We tend to mis-attribute others' behavior to personality, not context
- **Brené Brown's "The story I'm telling myself...":** A reframing tool for building empathy
- **Radical Candor (Kim Scott):** Challenging directly *and* caring personally

Reflect + Try This

- **Self-Check:** When I feel tension, do I start by blaming, or by asking questions?
- **Team Practice:** In a tense moment, pause and say: *"Let's reset, what's the intention here?"*
- **Leader Action:** Model vulnerability by naming a moment when your intent was misunderstood and how you clarified it.

Closing Thought

Assuming positive intent isn't about being passive; it's about being **proactive** with trust. It gives people room to be human, to grow, and to stay engaged even when things get hard.

The best teams don't avoid conflict. They face it with compassion. And it all starts with *how* we choose to see each other.

CHAPTER 4:

Yield to Creativity

"Creativity is intelligence having fun."
— *Albert Einstein*

What Is Creativity, Really?

CREATIVITY IS OFTEN mistaken for artistry, but it isn't limited to painters, musicians, or poets. At its core, creativity is the ability to generate ideas that are both novel *and* useful. It's about seeing connections others don't, asking "what if," and finding fresh ways through problems.

In business, this shows up everywhere:

- A strategist reframing a market challenge.
- An engineer hacking together a prototype.
- A leader shifting how a meeting starts.

Psychologists describe two key modes of thinking that fuel creativity:

- **Divergent thinking:** generating many possibilities, exploring without judgment.
- **Convergent thinking:** narrowing, refining, and choosing the best path forward.

Healthy teams move between the two, using tools like

brainstorming, mind-mapping, role-playing, and LEGO® SERIOUS PLAY® methods to stretch ideas wide, then sharpen them.

Together, these form the backbone of the **Creative Problem Solving (CPS) process**, pioneered by Alex Osborn (who coined *brainstorming*) and Sid Parnes. CPS has been taught for decades through the Creative Education Foundation and remains the foundation of much of today's **Design Thinking**.

The point is: creativity isn't random. It's not a lightning bolt reserved for geniuses. It's a process (a discipline) that anyone can learn, practice, and improve.

And here's the truth: while you may not think you're creative, you are. Every child doodles, imagines, builds, and questions. A famous study makes this clear. In 1968, George Land gave 1,600 children the same creativity test he had designed for NASA scientists. The results were startling: 98% of five-year-olds scored at the level of creative genius, but by age ten, it dropped to 30%, by fifteen to 12%, and in adults, just 2%. That spark doesn't disappear… it just gets buried under deadlines and doubt. Creativity is a muscle, not a mystery. The more we practice, the stronger it gets.

And how do we practice? Through play. Play lowers the stakes, fuels curiosity, and reawakens the creative wiring we've had since youth. When we make room for play, we make room for possibility.

Make Room to Wander

Creativity doesn't just appear, it has to feel **welcome**. Yet most teams say they value creativity while treating it like a luxury. It gets squeezed between deadlines, buried under bureaucracy, or boxed into a 30-minute brainstorming meeting between back-to-back Zoom calls.

We believe that creativity thrives where there's **permission to be messy, room to play, and a culture that celebrates possibility more than perfection.** Inviting creativity isn't about telling people to "think outside the box," it's about **redesigning the box** so they can breathe in it.

The Power of a Pivot

Change is the only constant in today's workplace. New technologies, shifting markets, surprise disruptions; they test every team's resilience.

Creativity is what makes pivots possible. When teams practice divergent thinking through play ("what if," "yes, and," "let's try") they rehearse flexibility. They get comfortable with novelty. And neuroscience tells us novelty releases dopamine, which sharpens attention and boosts learning.

Experiential learning cements this. When we physically act out an idea through improv, prototyping, or even playful art, we remember it more deeply than if we only discussed it.

Low-stakes play becomes a rehearsal space for change, building the toolkit we'll need when real disruption arrives.

In other words: creativity isn't just about new ideas. It's about adaptability. Variety trains flexibility. Play builds resilience. Creativity makes pivots possible.

The Da Vinci Principle

Leonardo da Vinci's notebooks weren't filled with polished masterpieces; they were chaotic. Half-finished sketches, absurd inventions, grocery lists, anatomical diagrams, philosophical questions. It was a safe space for creative chaos.

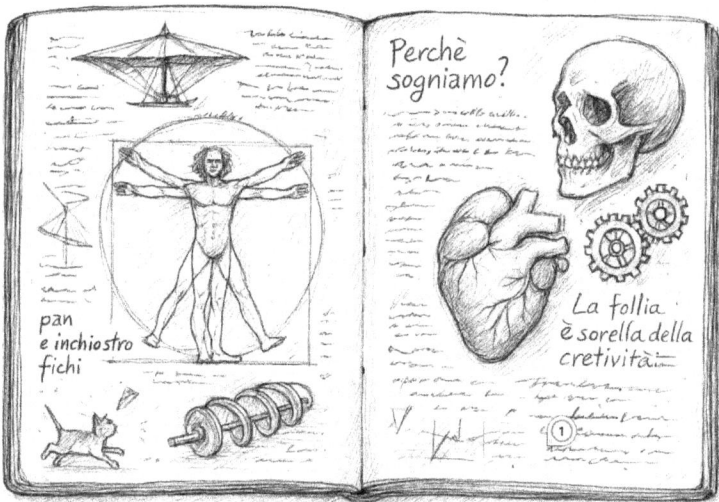

He invited creativity by staying curious. He paused. He wandered. He layered. Through that process, he bridged disciplines: art, science, engineering, anatomy and more. Da Vinci showed that Innovation happens at the intersections.

Centuries later, **Ada Lovelace** did the same with mathematics. Looking at Charles Babbage's analytical engine (a mechanical calculator), she imagined it composing music. Her creative leap reframed math as more than numbers: it was a canvas for invention, marking the birth of computer science and reminding us that creativity is what drives every breakthrough.

Decades after that, **Thomas Edison** carried this principle into practice at Menlo Park, building the first industrial R&D lab around the idea that failure was progress. He reframed 10,000 "failed" attempts not as waste, but as the path to light.

Da Vinci, Lovelace, and Edison remind us that creativity isn't magic; It's curiosity, discipline, and a willingness to welcome the messy middle. Every leap forward begins as an experiment.

Creative Cultures: Intersections at Play

The same principle doesn't just hold for individuals. It plays out collectively, too.

In 1919, the **Bauhaus school** in Germany tore down walls between art, architecture, and engineering. Painters studied furniture. Architects played with color. Metalworkers explored typography. The result was a movement that still shapes design today, because the culture invited cross-pollination.

Decades later, companies like **3M** and **Google** pioneered "15% time" and "20% time," letting employees pursue side projects. Out of that freedom came Post-it Notes, Gmail, and Google Maps.

Pixar built its headquarters around chance encounters: open atriums, shared cafés, hallways designed to spark collisions. As co-founder Ed Catmull put it, "Creativity doesn't follow job titles, it follows human connection."

And more recently, **Canva** introduced "Design Days," where employees step away from their roles to create, no outcomes required.

The throughline? Whether in Renaissance workshops,

German art schools, or Silicon Valley campuses, creativity doesn't happen by accident. It happens because leaders and cultures *invite it*.

Why Teams Need Creativity

Business leaders often claim creativity is a "nice to have." Research proves it's bottom-line strategy:

- **IBM Global CEO Study (2010)** surveyed 1,500 executives worldwide and found creativity was the single most important leadership quality for navigating complexity.

- **A McKinsey study (2020)** showed that companies embedding creativity into their strategy achieved 2x revenue growth compared to peers.

- **Neuroscience research** shows that when we engage in imaginative play, the brain's default mode network lights up, enhancing problem-solving and memory consolidation.

Creativity reduces burnout by reconnecting people with curiosity. It strengthens resilience by reframing failure as feedback. And it sparks innovation by turning "what is" into "what if."

If innovation is the engine, then inviting creativity is how we keep it fueled.

From Theory to Practice

Principle:

Make room for curiosity, imagination, and to wander.

Practice:

Designate "Wander Time" or "What If Hours"

Carve out space weekly or monthly for exploration. No agendas, no KPIs. This could mean team sketching, field trips, scavenger hunts, idea dumping, or collaborative creations.

Playful Ritual:

Creative Curiosities:

Reserve 5-10 minutes at the end of meetings to let your team share wild ideas, passions, or unexpected insights. Ask one person to start with a work-related (or not) win or spark. Whoever resonates says "pop" and adds their own quick connection. It keeps the momentum fast, playful, and surprising. You might start by saying,

- "I've been curious about how AI could help with brainstorming."
- "Pop! I used ChatGPT to draft a first version of a project plan."
- "Pop! Our team played with Midjourney to visualize a campaign idea."

No judgment. No follow-up required. Just shared imagination.

Application in Action

In one of our sessions, a sales team under pressure traded spreadsheets for imagination.

Instead of converging on what they already knew, we invited them into divergent thinking.

The challenge: in small groups, using only arts and crafts materials, create bold solutions to their biggest sales roadblocks. No budget. No rules. No reality required.

The room lit up. One team dreamed up a **sales teleporter** to connect instantly with clients. Another envisioned a **client crystal ball** to know exactly what customers *really* wanted. Laughter followed, but so did breakthroughs.

Amid the playful crafting came something real: a conversation about their struggle to gain credibility in a new industry. Using creative systems play, the team co-designed a practical path forward: leverage trusted clients and co-host pilot sessions with industry partners to open doors.

That moment turned pressure into progress. Within weeks, the team reignited a stalled account plan and exceeded their sales goals. Not because they followed a script, but because imagination helped them design a path forward.

Supporting Models & Theories

- **Psychological Capital (Luthans):** Hope, efficacy, resilience, optimism—creativity fuels them all
- **Divergent Thinking (Guilford, Torrance):** The foundation of ideation
- **Play Theory (Stuart Brown):** Play as the doorway to flow and imagination
- **Growth Mindset (Dweck):** Failure as feedback, creativity as capacity

Reflect + Try This

- **Self-Check:** When's the last time I made something? (Just for fun!)
- **Team Practice:** Hold a monthly "Play Break" where teams build, draw, act, or explore a shared challenge in an unusual way.
- **Leader Action:** Ask your team: *"Where are we leaving room for invention? And where are we accidentally stifling it?"*

Closing Thought

Creativity isn't reserved for artists. It belongs to the coder who rewrites a better script. The analyst who sees a new pattern. The facilitator who breaks up monotony with an impromptu dance party. When you invite creativity, you're saying:

Your imagination matters here. Innovation isn't just encouraged; it's embedded in who we are.

CHAPTER 5:

Invite Connection

"Connection is why we're here. It's what gives purpose and meaning to our lives."

— *Brené Brown*

Beyond Performance: The Power of Belonging

YOU CAN HAVE the smartest minds in the room, the sleekest tools, and the best-laid plans, but if your team doesn't feel connected to each other, it can all fall flat. **Connection isn't a bonus feature of healthy culture; it's a key ingredient.** And yet, many organizations treat it as a "soft skill," something to sprinkle in after the real work is done.

We like to flip that thinking on its head. Connection is purpose. **Connection *is* the work.** Because teams that trust each other innovate more, speak up, recover faster, and stay longer.

Ubuntu: A Timeless Lesson in Team Culture

There's an African philosophy called **Ubuntu**, which loosely translates to:

"I am because we are."

It's been a guiding principle in post-apartheid South Africa, community healing efforts, and even within competitive sports teams like the South African Rugby Union. What's the core idea?

We thrive through our relationships. We succeed by lifting each other up.

In the modern workplace, Ubuntu might look like pausing to ask how someone's really doing. Celebrating wins. Or offering help without needing a reason. Ubuntu is purposeful connection.

Connection in the Wild (and the Workplace)

A client of ours once described their culture as "efficient but lonely." Their remote team had Slack channels and Zoom meetings, but no *real* camaraderie… thanks in part to the pandemic. So, we led a virtual session where each person created a digital collage of their childhood dream job. They shared memories, laughter, and even poked fun here and there. Afterward, one participant shared: "I've worked with y'all for two years, and I feel like I finally really met you today."

Connection doesn't take long. It takes **intention.** And in healthy cultures, that intention shows up in the little things people say to one another:

"Thank you."

"How can I help?"

"You good?"

Those small signals carry big weight. They tell people they matter and that they don't have to go it alone.

Gratitude as a Connector

One of the simplest ways to act with intention is through gratitude.

Research from UC Davis psychologist Robert Emmons shows that gratitude practices increase resilience, strengthen relationships, and improve overall well-being. In the workplace, teams that regularly express gratitude report 50% higher engagement and lower turnover. Harvard Business Review notes that employees who receive recognition are four times more likely to be engaged than those who don't.

And gratitude doesn't have to be grand! It can be as simple as a genuine "thank you," a Slack shoutout, or ending a meeting by acknowledging someone's contribution. These small acts create belonging cues; signals that say, you matter here, we see you and we value you.

We've seen this firsthand time and time again. One of our ongoing clients began closing their weekly Friday meeting with a two-minute gratitude round. What started as quick acknowledgments soon became stories of support and appreciation. Within weeks, they weren't just working together, they were rooting for each other.

They weren't just working together, they were rooting for each other.

Connection deepens when gratitude is present. It transforms efficient teams into caring ones, and caring teams into powerful ones.

From Theory to Practice

Principle:

Build relationships, not just results.

Practice:

Make space for personal wins and shared gratitude.
Examples:

- **Meeting Moments:** Begin or end meetings with quick recognitions. Shoutout wins (of all sizes), small acts of support, or even moments of humor that lifted the team.
- **Highlight Reel:** End each week with a Teams or Slack thread where people post gratitude, fun photos, or little victories from the week. Weekly celebration.
- **Gratitude Wall:** Create a digital or physical wall where people can add sticky notes, doodles, or snapshots of appreciation. Sweeten it with playful rewards (random prize draws, coffee cards, or shoutouts from leadership).

Prompt:

"Who helped make your week easier, or brighter?"

Playful Ritual:

Shine Time

Once a month or at least 1x per quarter, host a 30-minute moment of appreciation and connection. The only items on the agenda: storytelling and recognition. Bonus points for props, emojis, or standing ovations. One fun idea to consider:

- Recognition Bingo:

    At the start of each month (or quarter), give team members a bingo card with simple recognition prompts (e.g., "Helped solve a problem," "Shared knowledge," "Brought positive energy," "Had my back this week"). As they notice these behaviors, they mark them off their card. At the monthly recognition meeting, shoutouts bring the cards to life. It's an easy, playful way to make gratitude a consistent habit.

Application in Action

A construction firm we work with was aiming to improve collaboration across departments. Field workers said they didn't feel respected by office staff, and office staff said they didn't feel heard by leadership... and so on.

We ran a LEGO® SERIOUS PLAY® workshop where everyone first built models of what "team success" looked like to them.

Big Surprise: The field team built bridges. The office team built hands passing batons. Leadership built scaffolding holding everyone up. It turned out, they weren't in conflict at all. They were simply using different metaphors for support.

After digging a bit deeper, we asked them to go one step further: build a model of gratitude for another part of the organization. The office team created models honoring the field team's long hours and problem-solving in tough conditions. Leadership built gratitude for the precision and persistence of both the office and field teams. The field crew expressed gratitude for leadership's vision and the office's behind-the-scenes coordination.

Gratitude became the turning point. It reframed frustrations as appreciation and gave people new language for respect. From there, the company launched an internal "Lunch & Learn" series where teams share workflows and tools; not just to teach, but to recognize each other's contributions.

Today, gratitude is woven into the fabric of their culture.

Recognition isn't reserved for once-a-year reviews; it's part of the everyday rhythm of work. A digital recognition board now captures daily micro-moments of appreciation, turning small gestures into shared wins. The result: stronger collaboration, deeper trust, and a workplace where *people consistently feel seen, heard, and valued.*

Supporting Models & Theories

- **Belonging Cues (Daniel Coyle):** Subtle signals that build trust and cohesion
- **Social Identity Theory (Tajfel & Turner):** We define ourselves through group affiliation
- **Psychological Safety (Amy Edmondson):** Stronger when people feel seen beyond their roles
- **Transformational Leadership:** Connection as the basis for influence and team loyalty

Reflect + Try This

- **Self-Check:** When was the last time I expressed appreciation to a colleague without a specific reason?
- **Team Practice:** Try a 'Get-to-Know-YOU' deck: each person adds a playful slide about themselves. (Think of it as a mini *Manual of Me*®.)
- **Leader Action:** Ask your team: *"What rituals make you feel part of something bigger?"* Then create space for them.

Closing Thought

Nurturing connection doesn't mean we slow down. It means we go further together.

Connection turns coworkers into collaborators. Teams into communities. Workplaces into cultures where people don't just survive; they belong.

And belonging isn't just a feeling. It shows up in the numbers. Research shows that a majority of employees have stayed at a job longer than expected because of workplace friendships, and more than 76% say they're more likely to stay when they feel real bonds at work. Friendship, recognition, and gratitude aren't "extras;" they're retention strategies.

The reason is simple: when people laugh together, play together, and know each other beyond their job titles, work becomes more than performance. It becomes personal. Gratitude builds respect. Play sparks joy. Shared stories create trust. Together, they form the glue for connection and belonging.

Because in the end, the best organizations aren't just built by people who work hard. They're built by people who care about the mission, and about each other. In other words, they're built by purpose, on purpose.

CHAPTER 6:

Normalize Reflection

"We do not learn from experience. We learn from reflecting on experience."

— *John Dewey*

The Fast-Paced Trap

IN TODAY'S PRODUCTIVITY-DRIVEN culture, reflection often gets treated like an option, something we'll do "when there's time." But time rarely makes itself available. So teams move faster, burn out quicker, and repeat the same mistakes in slightly more polished PowerPoints.

The alternative? Build reflection into the rhythm of your work. Normalize it. Ritualize it. Protect it. Because reflection isn't soft, it's strategic!

What you don't process, you repeat. What you reflect on, you can reimagine.

Stoics, Monks & Mastery

The idea of pausing to look inward (reflect) isn't new.

- The **Stoics** practiced evening reflections, reviewing not just what they did, but how they showed up: *"Where *did I act with courage? Where did I fall short? What will I do differently tomorrow?"*

- **Confucius** wrote, *"By three methods we may learn wisdom: first, by reflection, which is noblest..."* placing reflection above even experience itself.
- **Benjamin Franklin** kept a daily journal where he evaluated his 13 virtues, asking himself where he lived up to them and where he fell short.
- **Buddhist monks** journal about compassion and presence.
- **Athletes** watch film.
- **Artists** step back from the canvas & **Musicians** listen to their own recordings.

Across time and cultures, mastery doesn't come from moving faster. It comes from knowing when to pause and reflect.

Reflection in Organizations

Modern organizations have their own traditions of reflection:

- The U.S. Army's "After Action Reviews" has been credited with improving adaptability and resilience under pressure. They ask simple but powerful questions after every mission: *What was supposed to happen? What actually happened? Why were there differences? What can we learn?*
- In business, Agile retrospectives serve a similar function: pausing at the end of a sprint to ask what worked, what didn't, and what to try next. Research shows that teams who consistently hold retros have higher satisfaction and deliver better results.

- Harvard professor Francesca Gino found that employees who spent 15 minutes at the end of the day reflecting on what they learned performed 23% better after 10 days than those who didn't. Reflection literally accelerates growth.

From Theory to Practice

Principle:

Growth comes from looking inward and learning.

Practice:

Embed reflection points into every project, meeting, and milestone.

Ask questions like: *"What did we learn?"* and *"What would we do differently?"* every time; not just when something goes wrong.

End meetings with five minutes of silent reflection. Let people jot down insights, gratitude, or next steps. Give an option to share aloud, but no pressure. Just space.

Playful Ritual:
The Wall of Gratitude and Grievances

After a project or meeting, invite the team to reflect using sticky notes. On one side of a whiteboard label Gratitude and capture what went well and should be repeated. On the other side label Grievances. Then note what could have been better or done differently. Everyone contributes as many thoughts as they'd like. One thought per sticky, creating a colorful map of recognition, learning, and growth.

While it may feel risky to open the floor to grievances, in our experience it's exactly what many people are hoping for: a safe outlet to name frustrations. When surfaced constructively, those sticky notes often become cathartic moments of honesty that clear the air and move the team forward together, with a plan and shared purpose.

Application in Action

We worked with an agricultural business whose pace spiked during harvest season. For several months each year, the plant runs 24/7 to handle incoming crops and keep production moving.

The speed is relentless. Under that pressure, mistakes multiply: safety shortcuts, overlooked steps, and missed opportunities for improvement. In the past, those lessons were lost in the shuffle, and the same issues resurfaced with each new harvest. This time, leadership leaned into reflection, working with us to uncover insights and shape a different path forward before the next harvest.

We helped the team break that cycle by embedding reflection into the rhythm of the season.

- **Shift huddles** created space to share what was working and what wasn't, in real time.

- **Clock-off comments** captured daily ideas, frustrations, and small wins before they vanished.
- **End-of-season retrospectives** began with several divergent techniques (looking at you, *Wall of Gratitude and Grievances*) to surface every observation, then converged to organize and prioritize action.

The impact? Fewer repeated mistakes the following season. More small innovations were carried forward. And most importantly, a culture where reflection wasn't an afterthought; it was part of the work itself.

Supporting Models & Theories

- **Experiential Learning Cycle (David Kolb):** Reflection is required to convert experience into knowledge
- **Deliberate Practice (Anders Ericsson):** Progress demands feedback and pause
- **Self-Determination Theory (Deci & Ryan):** Reflection reinforces autonomy and meaning
- **Mindful Leadership (Harvard Business Review):** Regular reflection improves emotional regulation and decision quality

Reflect + Try This

- **Self-Check:** Do I pause after major moments, or rush into the next?
- **Team Practice:** At the end of each month, dedicate one team meeting to learning.
- **Leader Action:** Model reflection by sharing one learning from your week. Bonus points for modeling vulnerability if it came from a mistake.

Closing Thought

Reflection is not a detour from productivity. It's how we make meaning from motion.

To normalize reflection is to say:

We are not just here to execute. We're here to evolve. We don't just move forward; we grow forward.

And that's how true innovation begins: not in the rush, but in *the pause and reflection that gives it purpose.*

CHAPTER 7:

Name Your Impact

"In the end, we are all judged by the courage of our convictions, the strength of our ideas, and the measure of our impact."

— *Sheryl Sandberg*

Accountability ≠ Blame

SOMEWHERE ALONG THE way, *accountability* got a bad rap. It became code for punishment. For guilt. For "Who dropped the ball?" But in healthy teams, accountability is not about blame. It's about ownership. It's about understanding that every action (or inaction) sends ripples. The best cultures empower people not just to see those ripples, but to shape them intentionally.

At PlayInnové, we define it this way:

Ownership is a connection to the bigger result. And that connection sparks initiative, creativity, and courage. Once that connection is made, magic happens. People step up, speak out, and show what they're truly capable of.

Truman, Gandhi, and the Power of Responsibility

On President Harry Truman's desk sat a small sign: *"The Buck Stops Here."* He knew that leadership didn't mean passing blame; it meant owning outcomes, even when others had dropped the ball.

Across the globe, Mahatma Gandhi embodied a quieter version of the same principle. Though often paraphrased as *"Be the change you wish to see in the world,"* Gandhi consistently modeled this ethic, living with radical transparency and simplicity so his daily choices reflected the values he preached.

In the corporate world, Toyota pioneered the same spirit of ownership. In their production system, *any* worker on the assembly line had the authority to pull the Andon cord, stopping the line if they spotted a defect. Instead of punishment, this created shared responsibility. Quality wasn't just management's job; it belonged to everyone, at every level.

Ritz-Carlton brings that same principle from the production line to the front line. Every employee, from housekeeper to bellhop, receives a $2,000 "make-it-right" allowance to resolve guest issues instantly without waiting for managerial approval. The message is clear: each person owns the experience. Trust in individual judgment fuels exceptional service, customer loyalty, and pride in contribution.

Across politics, values, personal choice, and business practice, the lesson is the same: influence comes not from perfection, but from responsibility.

Why It Matters for Teams

A study in *Organizational Behavior and Human Decision Processes* found that when people take ownership of outcomes (even in group settings), performance, collaboration, and job satisfaction all increase.

Further research echoes this:

- **Gallup:** Teams with clear accountability are 27% more productive and 50% more likely to deliver above-average performance.
- **Harvard Business Review:** Leaders who model "extreme ownership" build trust and accelerate results.
- **Korn Ferry:** Cultures of accountability directly correlate with higher retention and engagement.

When accountability is shared, it creates *mutual momentum*. In contrast, unclear ownership often leads to:

- Finger-pointing
- Dropped deliverables
- Quiet quitting disguised as "someone else's job"

But when you build a culture of impact ownership, people shift from *"That's not my problem"* to *"How can I help move this forward?"*

Naming Matters

Naming has power. Psychologists tell us that labeling our emotions helps us process them. That's the genius of tools like Gloria Willcox's *Feelings Wheel*: when you name what you feel, it becomes more manageable.

The same is true for problems. There's an old saying in systems thinking: *naming the problem is half the battle*. Until you call something what it is, you can't design a solution. Naming both lightens the load and points the way forward.

So what about impact? When we name our purpose and impact (whether individual, team, or organizational) we move beyond vague intention. We own it. We embody it.

This is why we call this chapter Name Your Impact. Accountability isn't just about being responsible; it's about being visible. When people can point to the ripples they've created, they deepen both pride and responsibility.

The same principle scales to organizations. Companies that name their impact (sustainability reports, diversity dashboards, or community engagement) aren't just checking boxes. They're signaling to employees, customers, and stakeholders: *this is what we stand for, and this is where we're growing.* Research consistently shows that companies who report transparently on ESG (environmental, social, and governance) performance see higher trust and stronger brand value.

Naming isn't the end, it's the beginning. It turns accountability from abstract into concrete, from invisible into lived culture.

From Theory to Practice

Principle:

Take responsibility and celebrate contribution.

Practice:

Integrate "What I owned" into weekly check-ins.
Instead of just asking what people worked on, ask: *"What part of our success did you influence this week?"*

Prompt:

"How did my actions shape today's outcome, for better or worse?"

Playful Ritual:

The Rename Game

Create a rotating, tongue-in-cheek award (a toy crown, silly trophy, LEGO® build, or funny hat). Each week, the current holder passes it on to a teammate who modeled great ownership. But here's the twist:

- When handing it off, the giver must **name the impact** they saw:

  "This week, I'm renaming the award 'The Bridge Builder' because you connected two teams that weren't talking."

- The award takes on that name for the week, until it's passed again and renamed by the next person.

Over time, the award becomes a playful record of impact stories: a crown that's been "The Fire Extinguisher," "The Innovator," "The Glue," or "The Quiet Force." And because everyone knows they'll eventually have to hand it off, people stay on the lookout for moments of ownership to celebrate.

This ritual doesn't just reward impact, it creates a culture of noticing it, naming it, and passing it forward.

Application in Action

We worked with a small SaaS platform's leadership team to scope priorities for a new set of OKRs (Objectives and Key Results). We then invited the entire organization to openly discuss them and augment where necessary. Ownership has to be shared, not handed down.

Once the OKRs were ready, we turned them into a visual mind map on the wall in their break room, each objective placed inside a playful diagram for all to interact with. Then came the reflection: every employee was asked to name, in five words or fewer, how they or their role would contribute to each objective. Those short, identified commitments were added to the map, creating a colorful web of accountability that spanned every department and individual.

To take it further, we asked each person to design a small square, using materials of their choice, to represent their role's ownership of the OKRs. Some drew, others used watercolors, and some collaged. By the end, the squares formed a mosaic, unique in style but unified in purpose.

The process transformed OKRs from abstract leadership goals into a collective story. Employees didn't just see objectives on paper; they saw themselves in them. Reflection made the goals meaningful, and ownership made them real.

Supporting Models & Theories

- **Locus of Control (Rotter):** High internal control correlates with resilience and engagement
- **Radical Candor (Kim Scott):** Owning mistakes while caring personally

- **Psychological Ownership (Pierce et al.):** People commit more when they feel like something is "theirs"
- **Transformational Leadership:** Accountability paired with shared vision increases performance

Reflect + Try This

- **Self-Check:** When outcomes go sideways, do I look outward, or inward?
- **Team Practice:** End every project with a "What I Owned" and "What We Learned" conversation.
- **Leader Action:** Model public ownership of mistakes. It normalizes learning and builds credibility.

Closing Thought

When people **own their impact**, they stop waiting for permission to lead.

They step into possibility. They show up with intention. And they start to believe something radical: *My presence here matters.*

Because in every thriving team, the most powerful question isn't just *What's your role?* It's: *What kind of ripple are you choosing to create?*

CHAPTER 8:

Open to All Voices

*"Diversity is being invited to the party; inclusion
is being asked to dance."*

— *Verna Myers*

Innovation Starts with Who Gets Heard

IT'S NOT ENOUGH to gather a group of talented individuals and hope they collaborate. If only the loudest, most senior, or most dominant voices are consistently heard, you don't have a team, you have a performance.

To unlock real innovation, you need more than representation; you need **participation**. You need a culture where *every voice* feels valued, heard, and celebrated.

We've seen this play out in every industry, from tech to education to construction:

When inclusion is practiced (not just promised), trust deepens, ideas expand, and solutions get smarter.

A Global Lesson from a Local Council

In 2011, the city of Medellín, Colombia (once known for extreme violence) underwent a massive transformation. The catalyst? Not just funding or policy, but listening.

Leaders built community councils, made public transit free on Sundays, and moved city hall meetings into public libraries. They asked, *"What would make you feel safer?"* Then implemented what they heard.

This wasn't just civic planning; it was inclusion. And the results? Crime rates dropped. Public trust rose. The city was named *Innovative City of the Year* by *The Wall Street Journal*.

It's proof that people support what they help shape.

Medellín isn't alone! IDEO, the design firm that popularized design thinking, made "all voices in" a non-negotiable rule of brainstorming. Ideas are written first on sticky notes (before anyone speaks) so no voice gets overshadowed. The method has been replicated across industries, proving that innovation depends not on who speaks loudest, but on whether everyone is invited to speak at all.

Unfortunately, too often, the opposite happens. The HiPPO effect, short for the Highest Paid Person's Opinion, creeps into meetings and stifles creativity. When senior voices dominate, teams lose perspective, and innovation slows. The best ideas are often buried beneath hierarchy. Great leaders challenge the HiPPO by asking questions first, listening to diverse views, and creating psychological safety for others to contribute freely.

The Cost of Silence

According to research by Cloverpop, diverse teams make better business decisions 87% of the time, and inclusive teams are more likely to execute those decisions effectively. McKinsey's global research confirms it: companies in the top quartile for ethnic and gender diversity are up to 35% more likely to outperform financially. Deloitte found that inclusive teams are 80% more likely to report high performance.

And yet, silence persists. Studies also show that:

- Women are interrupted 33% more often than men in meetings.
- People of color report higher levels of code-switching and self-censorship.
- Neurodiverse team members are often misread, under-supported, or excluded from key conversations.
- Gallup found that employees who feel their voice is ignored are 4.6x more likely to feel disengaged.

Silence shows up in familiar ways: the idea never spoken because the meeting moved too fast. The junior staffer who lets a senior colleague claim their insight. The quiet engineer who shares brilliance only in a Slack DM after the fact.

The result? Missed insights, talent turnover, groupthink, and so on... Innovation doesn't fail from a lack of ideas; it fails from a lack of access to them.

From Theory to Practice

Principle:

Inclusion powers innovation.

Practice:

Rotate facilitation and share airtime intentionally.
Use tools like "Round-Robin Reflection" or "Chat Queueing" in hybrid meetings to invite different modes of input.

Prompt:

"Who haven't we heard from yet?" Then pause. Wait. Make space. Don't move on too fast.

Playful Ritual:

At the end of key meetings, invite the team to sketch a simple image of anything left unsaid on a sticky note: a concern, an idea, or a loose end. Each image is posted on a whiteboard upon exiting. At the beginning of the next meeting, a brief space is given to voice what was shared. It's a semi-anonymous way to gain ideas and challenges. It's not about extending the meeting; it's about closing the loop and making sure all perspectives are visible before moving forward.

Application in Action

At a niche commercial design firm we partnered with, the junior staff rarely spoke during brainstorming sessions. The leadership team was highly concerned by this and kept saying, "We want to hear your ideas!" but the very people with youthful, fresh perspectives weren't contributing out loud.

So, we shifted the format. Instead of another open-floor discussion, we invited everyone to build. Using LEGO® SERIOUS PLAY® methods, each person created a model of a recent idea to improve sales and attract new clients. The models told a story that the conversations never had. The fear of being wrong wasn't just holding back the junior team members; it was shared across the room at all levels.

What happened next was the real breakthrough. Because the models spoke for them, even the quietest voices were represented without fear. No one could dominate, no one could hide, and every perspective became visible. That 100% engagement carried into their daily culture. Soon, they added "Idea Labs" where all ideas could be surfaced; sometimes anonymously, always openly discussed, and credited generously.

Today, some of their best campaigns come from employees who, a year earlier, stayed silent in the back row. By making creativity tangible and playful, the team learned this truth: when every voice is invited to build, every voice is heard.

Supporting Models & Theories

- **Inclusive Leadership (Deloitte):** Belonging + uniqueness drives engagement
- **Groupthink Avoidance (Janis):** Diverse perspectives prevent tunnel vision
- **Psychological Safety (Edmondson):** A culture of respect and risk-taking
- **Equity-Centered Design (Creative Reaction Lab):** Who designs, who decides, who's affected?

Reflect + Try This

- **Self-Check:** Whose ideas do I tend to default to? Whose do I overlook?
- **Team Practice:** Assign a rotating "inclusion checker" at meetings; a person tasked with noticing who speaks and who doesn't.
- **Leader Action:** Publicly celebrate contributions that reflect unique perspectives, even when they push back or sound "out there."

Closing Thought

Valuing all voices doesn't mean every idea makes the final cut. It's about creating a culture where every contribution is welcomed with respect. Where people know:

"I'm not just here to fill a seat. I'm here because what I bring has value."

Because the best teams aren't defined only by what they produce, but by how they treat each other. They are the teams that nurture connection, normalize reflection, name their impact, and open the circle to every voice.

That's the heart of purpose: people working not just *with* each other, but *for* each other. And when purpose is alive, teams are ready for the next step: unlocking the spark of play that turns care into energy, resilience, and joy.

CHAPTER 9:

Value is Built with Yes, And

"Yes, and…" is more than a phrase. It's a posture. A way of saying: I hear you, I believe in your idea enough to build on it, and I trust this conversation isn't finished. It's just beginning.

Variety is the Spice of Life

HUMANS ARE WIRED for novelty. New sights, sounds, and experiences wake up our brains. Neuroscientists call this the **novelty effect**: when we encounter something different, dopamine fires, attention sharpens, and learning accelerates.

Yet, in many workplaces, variety is the first thing we cut. Meetings follow the same agenda, teams repeat the same patterns, and leaders default to the same voices.

Play offers an antidote. It creates safe, low-stakes opportunities to try something new, build on unexpected turns, and to embrace pivots. In play, we practice flexibility so that when real change comes (when the stakes are high) we already have the muscles to respond.

This is why "Yes, and…" matters. It's not just about laughter or improv games. It's about building cultures where variety isn't threatening, it's energizing! Where pivots aren't feared, they're practiced.

From Comedy Clubs to Boardrooms

The rule of "Yes, and…" comes from the world of improv comedy. In that context, it keeps a scene alive. One actor says, *"We're in a spaceship!"* and the other doesn't reply, *"No we're not."* They say, *"Yes, and there's a koala at the controls."* Laughter follows, not because of logic, but because of momentum.

But this isn't just for laughs. "Yes, and…" is a fundamental building block of **psychological safety** and **collaborative creativity.** In workplaces, it says:

"I won't shoot your idea down before it has a chance to breathe."

"I'll help us co-create, not compete."

"This is a space for possibility, we're not looking for perfection."

At PlayInnové, we use "Yes, and…" in everything from LEGO® SERIOUS PLAY® workshop warm-ups to strategy jams and change management sessions. It lowers the stakes and lifts the energy. And sometimes, the biggest breakthroughs are just one "Yes, and" away.

Historical Echoes of "Yes, And…"

The roots of improv trace back to 1920s immigrant neighborhoods in Chicago, where theater director Viola Spolin developed improvisational games for children in settlement houses. These were kids from dozens of cultures, learning English, negotiating differences, and finding common ground through play. Her simple exercises of "accept and build" became the foundation of what we now call improv.

In other words, "Yes, and" was born as a tool of inclusion. It wasn't about performance; it was about belonging.

History has other echoes of this principle:

Wartime collaboration and recovery (1940s): During World War II, British intelligence ran the Double-Cross System, turning enemy spies into double agents through careful, collaborative trust-building. After the war, that same spirit fueled the Marshall Plan, where nations said, "Yes, and let's rebuild together." What began as survival strategy became a blueprint for shared prosperity.

The birth of global community (1945): When 50 nations came together in San Francisco to form the United Nations, it would have been easy to splinter into competing agendas. Instead, they practiced "Yes, and" diplomacy, layering proposals into a shared charter that reflected possibility. The UN was built not from one voice, but from many combined.

Innovation under pressure (1970): When an oxygen tank exploded on Apollo 13, NASA engineers didn't waste time on blame. They built forward: "Yes, the system failed. And here's how we solve it with what we have." Their improvisation turned a likely tragedy into one of history's most celebrated rescues.

A lighter echo – the birth of jazz (1920s–30s): At the same time improv theater was taking shape, jazz musicians in Harlem and New Orleans were practicing their own "Yes, and." Each riff built on the last, mistakes became music, and collective creativity gave rise to an entirely new genre that transformed global culture.

"Yes, and" is how teams move from problems to possibility.

Why Teams Need "Yes, And"

Modern organizations often say they value innovation, but their habits tell another story. Meetings default to critique. Brainstorms become competitions. Conflict turns into blame.

"Yes, and" interrupts that cycle. It creates space for building rather than blocking. The truth is, value rarely comes from the first idea alone. It grows when one thought sparks another, when contributions layer into something stronger than any single voice. "Yes, and" is the posture that turns individual sparks into collective breakthroughs.

Research supports this:

- A study by **IDEO and the University of Chicago** found that teams using "Yes, and" techniques generated 28% more creative ideas than those who brainstormed without it.

- **Group creativity research (Keith Sawyer)** shows that improvisational collaboration (riffing, not resisting) is one of the strongest predictors of collective breakthroughs.

- **Harvard Business Review (2018)** highlighted improv training as a leadership tool, showing that leaders who practice "Yes, and" behaviors are rated higher in adaptability and communication.

The principle is simple:

- In meetings, "Yes, and" creates shared ownership of solutions.
- In brainstorming, it sparks unexpected brilliance.
- In conflict, it proves you can be collaborative even when you disagree.

Ideas need air. "Yes, and" expands. "No, but" contracts.

If innovation is oxygen, then "Yes, and" is the breath that keeps it flowing.

From Theory to Practice

Principle:

Build on ideas instead of blocking them.

Practice:

Yes, And Jam Sessions

Designate team time for "impossible ideas" where there are no critiques, only add-ons. Give sticky notes, markers, and music. Celebrate the absurd and see where it leads.

Prompt:

"What's one small addition that could build on this idea?"

Playful Ritual:

Begin every ideation session with a "Yes, and" warm-up

Split into pairs. One person makes a statement (serious or silly), and the other replies with "Yes, and…" then adds something. Do this for two minutes before real brainstorming begins.

This primes the brain for openness, collaboration, and low-stakes play. You may even find the warm-up delivers an idea worth keeping.

Application in Action

In one of our Art of Change workshops, a biotech team began by painting on their own canvases. Just as they started to feel ownership, the twist came: they had to pass their paintings to the person next to them. No explanations, very few instructions, and no control. Each layer built only on what was already there, guided by the simple prompt: "Yes, and…"

Announcing the shift was like raising the curtain! In an

instant, participants brought the classic drama of fight, flight, or freeze to life. Some froze in quiet panic, clamming up as they surrendered their work. Others lit up with relief, sprinting to pass off what they considered "mistakes" for someone else to tackle. And then there were the holdouts, negotiating for just a little more time before letting go.

But as the exercise continued, something shifted. The panic eased into curiosity. The resistance gave way to trust. The group began to see that what felt uncomfortable at first was actually an invitation to adapt and build. By the end, the room buzzed with discovery:

"I really didn't enjoy giving up control over the canvas I started. It reminded me I need to be mindful when delegating."

"I didn't realize how often I block ideas before they even land."

"This reminded me that collaboration means trusting the process, not perfecting the outcome."

The canvases themselves became abstract masterpieces: messy, surprising, and beautiful. But the real masterpiece came later: a few weeks after the workshop, the team launched an initiative that had been stalled for six months. The only change? They began using *"Yes, and"* in every planning meeting.

Supporting Models & Theories

- **Design Thinking (IDEO):** Divergent > Convergent thinking
- **Group Flow (Keith Sawyer):** Collective creativity emerges when people riff, not resist
- **Improv in Leadership (Harvard Business Review):** Agility and responsiveness stem from co-creation
- **Growth Mindset (Carol Dweck):** "Yes, and" embraces the journey of evolving ideas

Reflect + Try This

- **Self-Check:** Do I naturally block or build?
- **Team Practice:** Set a 7-minute timer in your next meeting where every response must begin with "Yes, and..."
- **Leader Action:** In tough conversations, model possibility. Instead of correcting, ask: *"Yes, and how might we solve that together?"*

Closing Thought

"Yes, and" doesn't mean agreeing with everything. It means **inviting expansion**, exploration, and co-authorship.

In a world that often defaults to critique, "Yes, and" is a revolutionary kindness. It tells your team:

- Your voice belongs here.
- Your ideas matter.
- We're in this together.

And that's where value is built: not in one idea, but in the layering of many. When variety is embraced and contributions compound, teams don't just survive change; they thrive through it.

CHAPTER 10:

Energize the Work

*"A business has to be involving, it has to be fun,
and it has to exercise your creative instincts."*
— *Richard Branson*

Work Can Be a Playground, Even When It's Hard

LET'S GET THIS out of the way: *Energizing the work* doesn't mean turning every meeting into karaoke or pretending your quarterly report is a Pixar film. It means **reconnecting people to the fuel behind the function**: joy, purpose, play, meaning.

It means asking, *"What makes this worth showing up for?"* and then building culture around that. When work is energized, it doesn't just get done; it gets done with **aliveness.**

The Walt Disney Debrief

Walt Disney was known for sparking imagination in informal settings, often over lunches with his Imagineers where artists, engineers, and storytellers tossed around ideas freely. No pressure, just play. He believed magic didn't happen in the boardroom. We now see it happened in the margins, where people felt safe to dream, laugh, and experiment.

And here's the key: this wasn't just Walt's charisma. Personality hires and "fun leaders" can spark moments, but sustainable cultures don't rely on personalities, they rely on practices. The lesson isn't "be Walt," it's "build Walt-like spaces" where imagination is expected, not exceptional.

Pixar later carried that same spirit forward with *Notes Day* (2014), when the entire studio paused normal work to brainstorm how Pixar itself could work better. From animators to accountants, everyone's input mattered. The event didn't just generate process improvements; it re-energized employees by showing that their voices carried weight.

History offers more echoes. Thomas Edison hosted "invention picnics" at Menlo Park, where food, music, and playful tinkering fueled breakthroughs. Southwest Airlines built a culture where employees were encouraged to bring humor and personality into their roles. This energized not just their teams but millions of passengers.

Across industries and eras, the lesson is the same: energized work often emerges not in rigid structures, but in the margins where people feel free to bring joy, imagination, and aliveness into what they do.

Why Energy Matters in the Workplace

Research confirms what history suggests: energy fuels performance.

- **Gallup meta-analysis of 1.4M employees (2020):** Energized, engaged workers are 21% more productive, 41% less likely to miss work, and 23% more profitable for their companies.
- **McKinsey (2021):** Only about 15% of employees globally report feeling "truly engaged." The gap isn't about output; it's about energy alignment.

- **Harvard Business Review (Cross, 2016):** Networks with *energizing interactions* consistently outperform those dominated by neutral or draining ones.
- **MIT Human Dynamics Lab (Pentland, 2012):** The three most important predictors of team success are energy, engagement, and exploration.

In other words: productivity is not just about time or talent. It's about whether people feel energized in the work itself. When energy is present, performance compounds. When it's missing, even the smartest strategy can fall flat.

Energy at Work: What Teams Feel

The research is clear, but we've also seen it firsthand: energy is contagious.

- A drained leader can walk into a room and watch motivation evaporate.
- A playful spark like a joke, a creative exercise, or a simple moment of recognition can shift an entire team's posture.
- Sustained energy doesn't come from constant hype; it comes from weaving joy and meaning into the work itself.

High-energy teams don't mean loud teams. They mean aligned teams, where people feel like their effort and ideas matter, and their presence makes a difference.

That's the heart of energizing the work: designing cultures where energy isn't left to chance, but becomes part of the system.

From Theory to Practice

Principle:

Make it meaningful, joyful, and worth showing up for.

Practice:

Co-create purpose and permission to play.
Ask your team:

- *What lights you up here?*
- *Where do you feel most in flow?*
- *What do we need more fun around?*

Build micro-moments of celebration and ownership into the day-to-day.

Prompt:

"What's one way we can bring more joy or meaning into this project?"

Playful Ritual:

Play Breaks

Sometimes the fastest way to refuel isn't more coffee or another checklist... it's play! Energizers, or "Play Breaks," are intentional pauses that reset energy, spark creativity, and reconnect people to each other. They don't take long, but they shift the room.

For Culture:

Make play part of the fabric of the organization.

- **Annual Play Day:** A company-wide event with creative challenges, collaborative builds, and lighthearted competitions.

- **Failure Festival:** Celebrate learning by sharing (and perhaps laughing at) mistakes together, reframing failure as fuel. To make it land, leaders must go first and model vulnerability. Keep it light! The goal isn't roasting, it's normalizing risk-taking and reminding people that failure isn't fatal. It's fuel.
- **Creative Collage Walls:** Invite employees to contribute sketches, quotes, or ideas to a growing, visible canvas that celebrates imagination across the company.

For Teams:

In group settings, Play Breaks help balance focus with fun.

- **Impromptu Dance Party:** Play a song and let the team move for two minutes. No choreography required, just laughter and movement.
- **Desk Safari:** Everyone snaps a playful photo using whatever's nearby (a stapler as binoculars, a notebook as a hat), then shares in Slack/Teams or in the room.
- **One-Minute Masterpiece:** With markers, LEGO® Bricks, or sticky notes, everyone creates a lightning-fast "masterpiece" in response to a playful prompt ("What's your favorite thing about this team?").

For Individuals & Meetings:

Even micro-moments can bring energy back into the work.

- **Playful Check-Ins:** Open with a creative question like, "What emoji matches your mood today?" or "If this project were a movie, what's the title?"
- **Silent Build & Share:** Give two minutes for a quick LEGO® bricks build or doodle that answers a reflective

prompt ("What's one strength I'm bringing to this meeting?").

- **Brain Refresh:** Toss out a playful metaphorical question mid-meeting to spark perspective-shifting answers.

Bonus: Keep the Creativity Flowing

For individuals and teams who want a little more structure, we also recommend leaning on creative resources designed to spark fresh thinking:

- *Creative Thinker's Exercise Book* by Dorte Nielsen & Katrine Granholm
- *Creativity Workout* by Edward de Bono

Both are filled with short, practical exercises you can use on your own or with a group.

These aren't gimmicks. They're design. Play breaks make energy renewable, reminding teams that when we laugh, create, or even fail together, we recharge the fuel that makes the real work possible.

Application in Action

At a mid-sized logistics company, leadership told us: *"Our people are tired of monotony, but we don't know how to fix it."*

We designed a half-day experience using watercolor and creative storytelling. The goal? Help the team reconnect to why they do what they do. And, what makes them feel most alive while doing it.

During one reflection exercise, a participant admitted: *"I realized I haven't celebrated a win in months. Not even mine. Just… moving on to the next thing."* That moment became the spark.

Together, the group co-designed new energy rituals:

- A monthly "Win Wall" for capturing and celebrating successes.
- 3-minute creative reset breaks in long meetings.
- Peer-nominated recognition award, "The Sunshine Award" for moments of enthusiasm, excitement, and contagious positivity.

Three months later, turnover dropped. Energy lifted. People started showing up early, not because they had to, but because they wanted to. Reflection gave them clarity. Ownership gave them momentum. And energy gave them back their spark.

Supporting Models & Theories

- **Job Crafting (Wrzesniewski & Dutton):** Reshaping work to make it more meaningful
- **Flow Theory (Csikszentmihalyi):** Deep focus and joy increase creativity and output
- **Intrinsic Motivation (Deci & Ryan):** Autonomy, mastery, and purpose drive engagement
- **Play Theory (Stuart Brown):** Play is biologically essential for innovation and adaptability

Reflect + Try This

- **Self-Check:** What part of my work gives me energy, and what drains it?
- **Team Practice:** Run a "This Gives Me Life" roundtable: each person shares a task or moment that energizes them. Then design projects accordingly.
- **Leader Action:** Bake energy checks into 1:1s. Ask: *"What would bring more aliveness to your role this month?"*

Closing Thought

Energizing the work isn't a luxury. It's a leadership strategy. It's how we tap into what makes teams not just function, but **flourish.**

Because when people feel energized, they take initiative. They collaborate better. They bounce back faster. And most importantly, they **remember why they care.**

In the end, the best workplaces don't just get results.

They *spark something bigger.*

They leave people better than they found them.

They feel... *alive.*

CHAPTER 11:

Adaptive Advantage

(Why Play Belongs at the Center of Culture)

Play Is Not a Perk

I F YOU ASK a child why they play, they won't say, *"To improve my executive function,"* or *"To strengthen my resilience."* They'll shrug and say, *"Because it's fun."*

LOOK MOMMY! WE PLAY TO LEARN AND STRENGTHEN OUR RESILIENCE!

...SAID NO CHILD EVER.

But neuroscience, evolutionary biology, and decades of organizational research agree: play is far more than fun. It's how humans (and nearly every mammal) **learn, adapt, and survive.**

- **Lion cubs** wrestle not because they're bored, but to practice hunting.
- **Rats** deprived of play in youth grow into anxious, less adaptable adults. Jaak Panksepp, who identified the brain's "play circuit," demonstrated that play is hardwired into mammalian survival.
- **Children** with more unstructured playtime develop stronger problem-solving skills, emotional regulation, and social intelligence.

And yet, somewhere between recess and our first office job, play was stamped *"not serious."* We traded it for productivity hacks, endless meetings, and efficiency dashboards.

Here's the paradox: in stripping play from work, we stripped out the very thing that makes work productive in the first place.

The Strategic Case for Play

The evidence is clear: play isn't a side note; it's a strategy. Organizations that deliberately carve out space for curiosity and experimentation don't just generate ideas; they generate measurable results. From breakthrough products to resilient cultures, play has been the quiet engine behind some of the most iconic business successes.

The business case is undeniable:

- **Deloitte Human Capital Trends** report found that organizations with strong cultures of curiosity and experimentation outperform peers in both revenue growth and innovation.
- **Gallup's State of the Global Workplace (2025)** shows that only 21% of employees worldwide feel engaged in their work. Play fosters the belonging and joy that engagement metrics are crying out for.

- **Harvard Business Review** linked humor and play at work to increased psychological safety, the single strongest predictor of team innovation and retention.

Play isn't "extra." It's ROI.

Why Play Outperforms Pressure

We've been sold the myth that **pressure produces diamonds.** That stress, deadlines, and fear are what sharpen performance.

The reality? Too much pressure produces burnout, mistakes, and turnover.

Play offers the opposite:

- It lowers fear so people take smarter risks.
- It opens divergent thinking so new ideas emerge.
- It creates belonging cues so people stay and contribute.

And critically, play gives us a rehearsal space for pivots. In low-stakes settings, teams practice adaptability, novelty, and letting go of control. When real disruption hits, they already have the muscles to respond. When play is woven into culture, the results *are* measurable: higher engagement, more innovation, and faster recovery from setbacks.

Case Studies: Proof in Practice

- At Atlassian, engineers were encouraged to take quarterly "ShipIt Days." 24-hours to work on any idea they chose. Many playful prototypes became core product features, proving that a little structured freedom sparks real innovation.
- LEGO®, after facing near-bankruptcy in the early 2000s, leaned into play internally by inviting employees to experiment with small, low-stakes design sprints. This

culture of creative iteration helped revive the brand and set the stage for global growth.

- Zappos built a culture where playful rituals, from costume parades to spontaneous desk games, weren't distractions but belonging cues. The result: one of the lowest turnover rates in retail and a reputation for legendary customer service.

These aren't accidents. They're outcomes of leaders deliberately making space for curiosity, experimentation, and yes, play.

The Neuroscience of Play

Play isn't just cultural, it's biological.

- It activates dopamine, the brain's motivation and learning fuel.
- It increases neuroplasticity, strengthening new pathways for creativity and problem-solving.
- It lowers cortisol, reducing stress and building resilience.
- Novelty, the lifeblood of play, sharpens attention and accelerates learning.

In other words… play primes the brain for the very things leaders say they want more of: creativity, focus, agility, and innovation.

Busting the Myths

- **Myth:** Play wastes time.

  Reality: Play reduces wasted time by sparking faster breakthroughs.
- **Myth:** Play is for kids.

Reality: Play is how all mammals (humans included) learn, bond, and adapt.

- Myth: Play means chaos.

Reality: Structured play creates *safety* for experimentation without high-stakes risk.

From Theory to Practice

Play isn't theoretical, it's tactical.

Throughout this book, we've shared micro-moments of play: the *Feelings Wheel* check-in (Chapter 1), *Listen + Reflect* rounds (Chapter 2), *Curiosity Circles* (Chapter 3), gratitude rituals (Chapter 5), *Yes, And* warm-ups (Chapter 9), and so on...

But what if you want to go further? What if you want play to be not just a moment, but a muscle?

Practical Toolkit: How to Play at Work (Without Looking Silly)

Here are ways we've seen play change energy, connection, and performance in real organizations:

Energizers & Rituals

- *Two-Minute Dance Party* → Reset energy in the middle of a long day.
- *The Failure Game* → Celebrate one "fail" of the week, and the lesson it taught.
- *Wander Questions* → "If this project were an animal, what would it be?"
- *Desk Safari* (remote-friendly) → Use everyday objects to create and share a funny photo.

From the PlayInnové Toolkit

- **LEGO® SERIOUS PLAY® Methods** for trust, story-telling, and collaboration.

- **The Art of Change** acrylic workshops for resilience and adaptation.
- **Mindful Watercolor** breaks to pair pause with creativity.
- **Living Mandalas** to visualize collective values.

DIY for Leaders & Facilitators

- **Start small:** a one-word check-in is play.
- **Model it:** if leaders play, others will too.
- **Make it regular:** culture shifts through weekly rituals, not annual off-sites.
- **Tailor it:** match the play to your people. Some thrive on art, others on movement, others on story.

Reflect + Try This

- **Self-Check:** When was the last time I played for no reason other than joy?
- **Team Practice:** Assign a rotating "Play Master" to bring a 5-minute energizer to weekly meetings.
- **Leader Action:** Run a pilot "Play Break" for your team. Notice what shifts when play becomes rhythm, not exception.

Closing Thought

Play isn't the opposite of work. It's the opposite of disengagement.

When leaders treat play as a serious strategy, teams don't just perform better... they become more human. They adapt faster, collaborate deeper, and recover stronger.

If you ever wonder whether it's working? Just look around.

If people are so engaged they forget to check their phones, you've tapped into something real.

The future won't belong to the teams with the most rigid processes or the shiniest tools. It will belong to the teams who remember how to explore, to connect, and to play.

CHAPTER 12:

Venturing Ahead Together

"In times of change, learners inherit the earth."
— *Eric Hoffer*

Advancing Together

THE FUTURE OF work isn't approaching in the distance. It's already here.

Artificial intelligence is reshaping how we think about productivity. Remote and hybrid models have redrawn the map of collaboration. Climate shifts, demographic transitions, and constant disruption are now the backdrop of our professional lives.

And yet, the story of tomorrow won't be written by organizations that invest only in the latest software, restructure for efficiency, or cling to rigid strategies. It will be written by the leaders and teams who know how to adapt together.

Looking Back to Look Ahead

Throughout this book, we've explored practices that may have felt deceptively small at first: pausing at the start of a meeting, listening generously, assuming positive intent, inviting creativity, or sharing gratitude. But the truth is, these "small" moves are the most powerful levers of all.

- Pause clears the noise and resets focus.
- Listening opens the door for ideas and untapped voices.
- Gratitude transforms efficiency into belonging.
- Creativity reframes disruption as possibility.
- Ownership turns vague intention into meaningful purpose and impact.
- Play weaves these practices together, making culture feel alive, energizing, and worth showing up for.

Individually, they matter. But woven together, they form a living compass. A way of working that makes teams not just effective, but resilient and connected.

Adaptability as the Edge

If there's one capability the future demands, it's adaptability. Technologies will evolve, markets will shift, and surprises will arrive without warning. The question isn't if disruption will come, but how we will respond when it does.

Rigid systems crumble under pressure. But cultures that practice reflection, encourage experimentation, and make play part of the rhythm are ready. They know how to pivot without panic, how to collaborate instead of compete, and how to treat failure not as shame but as feedback.

Adaptability doesn't emerge by accident. It grows from repetition: tiny rituals that rehearse resilience long before the stakes are high.

Leadership for a Human Future

Leading in this era means more than setting goals or tracking performance. It means modeling the courage to pause when everyone else is rushing. It means making space for every voice, not just the loudest. It means designing work that is human, not just efficient.

As leaders, we have both the opportunity and the responsibility to create environments where people feel safe to experiment, energized to contribute, and connected to each other. That doesn't mean every moment will be easy. But it does mean every moment has the potential to teach, to build trust, and to move us forward.

The Power of Daily Culture

Culture isn't built in a single workshop, offsite, or keynote. It's built in the small daily actions: the decision to open with gratitude, the laughter shared in the middle of pressure, the courage to pause when urgency takes over.

Every moment is a choice. A chance to either reinforce disengagement or to build connection. To cling to control or to create belonging. To play it safe, or to play toward possibility.

That's the real invitation: to see culture not as something abstract, but as something alive. Something shaped by the choices and practices we repeat, day after day.

Closing Thought

The future won't be inherited by the strongest or the fastest. It will belong to those who adapt with courage, connect with intention, and never lose sight of the power of presence, purpose, and play.

So here's the choice before us:

Do we wait for change to happen to us?

Or do we create cultures that are ready to meet tomorrow, today?

EPILOGUE:

Your Invitation

WHAT YOU'VE READ in these pages isn't a prescription, it's a set of possibilities. Small practices that you can bring into your work as often or as lightly as you choose.

A pause at the start of a meeting.

A moment of gratitude in the middle of pressure.

A playful reset when energy dips.

An open question that makes space for a quieter voice.

Individually, these may feel like micro-actions. But practiced consistently, they create macro impact. They build trust. They strengthen connection. They transform how teams show up... not with more effort, but with more intention.

The future of work will always be uncertain. New challenges, shifting markets, accelerating change. But the tools to meet it are here, in the choices you make every day. How you respond. How you listen. How you invite others to step in and share.

The invitation isn't to overhaul everything at once. It's to begin where you are. Pick one practice. Try it. Notice what shifts. Then build from there.

Because the next chapter doesn't live in this book. It lives in your team.

In your next conversation.

Your next experiment.

Your next brave pause.

So go on! Make the small moves that spark big change.

And don't forget to pause, make purposeful connections, and play!

ACKNOWLEDGMENTS

THIS BOOK WAS never built alone. It is a mosaic of people, ideas, conversations, experiences, and sparks that found each other over time.

To the *teams* that let us into their stories, struggles, and LEGO® piles, you brought the writing to life. Your openness, playfulness, and willingness to try something different make this book for you.

To our early workshop participants, thank you for testing messy ideas with enthusiasm and grace. You helped refine pause, purpose, and play before it had a name.

To the mentors, facilitators, educators, and play practitioners whose work paved the way, thank you for reminding the world that fun and depth can (and must) coexist.

To our families and chosen families: your belief sustained this book through long days, playful interruptions, and unexpected turns.

And to you, dear reader, thank you for picking up this book. Thank you for caring enough to want something better for your team. Thank you for believing that work can be both purposeful *and* playful.

Here's to the builders.

The bridge-makers.

The brave listeners.

The culture cultivators.

The ones who say yes to change, and "yes, and" to each other. Let's play it forward!

ABOUT THE AUTHORS

VANYA BOARDMAN IS a leadership facilitator, storyteller, and co-founder of PlayInnové, known for using creative play to help teams spark fresh ideas and build trust. She brings two decades of leadership experience in business and facilities operations, working across financial services, telecom, health tech, and commercial real estate. She adds real-world insight to every workshop and story she shares. Vanya earned her master's in management and leadership from Pepperdine University and her bachelor's in business administration and marketing. Originally from Tacoma, WA, she now lives in sunny San Diego with her husband and two teens. When she's not leading energetic, hands-on workshops, you'll find her recharging with books, creating art, hiking, or exploring new locations with her family.

AUSTIN ROBERTS IS a creative consultant, facilitator, and co-founder of PlayInnové, known for blending creative play with people-centered strategy to help teams collaborate and innovate. He has supported leaders through culture-building, engagement work, and organizational development. Austin earned his master's in management and leadership from Pepperdine University and his bachelor's degree from the University of the Pacific. Austin loves the outdoors, discovering new foods, and traveling to experience life through fresh lenses. His passion for nature and sustainability continues to shape his work and worldview. You'll often find him on a trail with his dogs, Duke and Baron, or in a research rabbit hole with his cat nearby.

RESOURCES
(by chapter)

Introduction

"From an evolutionary perspective, play is how mammals, including humans, first learn..."

- Burghardt, G. M. (2005). The genesis of animal play: Testing the limits. MIT Press.
- Piaget, J. (1962). Play, dreams and imitation in childhood. W. W. Norton & Company.

"Play regulates stress, strengthens relationships, and helps us adapt better."

- Brown, S., & Vaughan, C. (2009). Play: How it shapes the brain, opens the imagination, and invigorates the soul. Avery.

"Play lowers fear so people take smarter risks."

- Sutton-Smith, B. (2001). The ambiguity of play. Harvard University Press.

"Play fosters psychological safety, the belief that employees at all levels can share ideas..."

- Edmondson, A. C. (2019). The fearless organization: Creating psychological safety in the workplace for learning, innovation, and growth. Wiley.

"Play reinforces a culture of continuous learning through experimentation and exploration."

- Mainemelis, C., & Ronson, S. (2006). Ideas are born in fields of play: Towards a theory of play and creativity in organizational settings. Research in Organizational Behavior, 27, 81–131. https://doi.org/10.1016/S0191-3085(06)27003-5

"When teams play well, they… reduce burnout, retain talent, and innovate with more joy and less friction."

- Schaufeli, W. B., & Bakker, A. B. (2004). Job demands, job resources, and their relationship with burnout and engagement: A multi-sample study. Journal of Organizational Behavior, 25(3), 293–315. https://doi.org/10.1002/job.248
- Fredrickson, B. L. (2001). The role of positive emotions in positive psychology: The broaden-and-build theory of positive emotions. American Psychologist, 56(3), 218–226. https://doi.org/10.1037/0003-066X.56.3.218

Chapter 1: Presence with Purpose

"Attention is the rarest and purest form of generosity."

- Weil, S. (1952). Gravity and Grace (E. Crawford & M. von der Ruhr, Trans.). Routledge & Kegan Paul. (Original work published 1947).

"A Harvard study on mindfulness at work showed that even brief presence practices improve focus and reduce stress by up to 30%."

- Dane, E., & Brummel, B. J. (2014). Examining workplace mindfulness and its relations to job performance and turnover intention. Human Relations, 67(1), 105–128. https://doi.org/10.1177/0018726713487753

"Aristotle's students earned the nickname Peripatetics – 'those who walk about,' because he taught while strolling in the gardens."

- Britannica. (n.d.). Peripatetic | philosophy. Encyclopedia Britannica. https://www.britannica.com/topic/Peripatetic

"Beethoven carried sketchbooks on hikes, capturing melodies that emerged from the stillness of nature."

- Im Freien. (2017). Beethoven und die Natur. Beethoven-Haus Bonn. https://www.beethoven.de/en/node/254844

"Steve Jobs made walking meetings a habit, a practice Tim Cook and other CEOs still carry on."

- Levy, S. (2017). The Oral History of Apple Infinite Loop. Wired. https://www.wired.com/story/apple-infinite-loop-oral-history/
- Mossberg, W. (2017). Tim Cook on shaping the future of Apple. GQ. https://www.gq.com/story/tim-cook-on-shaping-the-future-of-apple

"Even Winston Churchill, under wartime pressure, found grounding in painting and reflective walks..."

- Keegan, J. (2004). Leadership lessons from history: Winston Churchill during World War II. The Independent Institute.
- Manchester, W., & Reid, P. (2012). The Last Lion: Winston Spencer Churchill, Defender of the Realm 1940–1965. Little, Brown and Company.

"Modern neuroscience affirms this: intentional presence activates brain networks tied to creativity..."

- The Decision Lab. (n.d.). Cognitive load theory. https://thedecisionlab.com/reference-guide/psychology/cognitive-load-theory
- PositivePsychology.com. (n.d.). Flow state theory. https://positivepsychology.com/mihaly-csikszentmihalyi-father-of-flow/

"Exploring the Relationship Between Creativity Training and the Practice of Pause for Leaders..."

- Ralph, S. M., Jr. (2017). Exploring the relationship between creativity training and the practice of pause for leaders in a world of information overload (Doctoral dissertation, Pepperdine University). ProQuest Dissertations Publishing.

"Using Gloria Willcox's Feelings Wheel as a guide..."

- Willcox, G. (1982). The Feeling Wheel. Self-published tool for emotional awareness. Reproduced and widely distributed in therapeutic and educational contexts. See overview: Positive Psychology. (2020). Emotion Wheel. https://positivepsychology.com/emotion-wheel/

"Supporting Models & Theories: Cognitive Load Theory, Emotional Contagion Theory, Flow State Theory, Mindful Leadership

- Hatfield, E., Cacioppo, J. T., & Rapson, R. L. (1994). Emotional contagion. Cambridge University Press.
- Csikszentmihalyi, M. (1990). Flow: The psychology of optimal experience. Harper & Row.
- Carroll, M. (2008). The mindful leader: Awakening your natural management skills through mindfulness meditation. Shambhala Publications.
- Goleman, D. (2012, October). Mindfulness helps you become a

better leader. Harvard Business Review. https://hbr.org/2012/10/
mindfulness-helps-you-become-a

Chapter 2: Listen Generously

"Most people do not listen with the intent to understand; they listen
with the intent to reply."

- Covey, S. R. (1989). The 7 habits of highly effective people: Powerful
  lessons in personal change. Free Press.

"FDR's Fireside Chats shaped by listening to public concerns..."

- National Archives. (n.d.). Fireside Chats. https://www.archives.gov/
  milestone-documents/fireside-chats

"Mandela's lessons from village councils—leaders speak last."

- Mandela, N. (1994). Long walk to freedom: The autobiography of
  Nelson Mandela. Little, Brown and Company

"Quaker clearness committees and Indigenous talking circles."

- Friends General Conference. (n.d.). Clearness Committees. https://
  www.fgcquaker.org/
- Native American Rights Fund. (n.d.). Circle practices. https://narf.
  org

"MIT's Human Dynamics Lab found team listening predicts success."

- Pentland, A. (2012). The new science of building great teams.
  Harvard Business Review, 90(4), 60–69.

"Google's Project Aristotle identified psychological safety as key."

- Duhigg, C. (2016, February 25). What Google learned from its quest
  to build the perfect team. The New York Times Magazine. https://
  www.nytimes.com/2016/02/28/magazine/what-google-learned-from-
  its-quest-to-build-the-perfect-team.html

"McKinsey linked inclusive listening with higher performance."

- McKinsey & Company. (2020). Diversity wins: How inclusion
  matters. https://www.mckinsey.com/featured-insights/
  diversity-and-inclusion/diversity-wins-how-inclusion-matters

"Neuroscience shows humans are wired to connect through listening."

- Lieberman, M. D. (2013). Social: Why our brains are wired to connect. Crown.

Chapter 3: Assume Positive Intent

"Mandela's reconciliation after prison set a global example."

- Mandela, N. (1994). Long walk to freedom: The autobiography of Nelson Mandela. Little, Brown and Company.

"Attribution bias often skews intent; reframing tools help."

- Brown, B. (2015). Rising strong. Spiegel & Grau.
- Scott, K. (2017). Radical candor: Be a kick-ass boss without losing your humanity. St. Martin's Press.
- Frei, F., & Morriss, A. (2020). Begin with trust. Harvard Business Review, 98(5), 112–119.
- Heider, F. (1958). The psychology of interpersonal relations. Wiley.

"IBM's 2010 CEO Study ranked creativity the top leadership quality."

- IBM. (2010). Capitalizing on complexity: Insights from the global chief executive officer study. IBM Global Business Services. https://www.ibm.com/downloads/cas/1VZV5X8J
- Dignan, L. (2010, May 18). IBM's CEO study: Creativity top leadership quality. ZDNet. https://www.zdnet.com/article/ibms-ceo-study-creativity-top-leadership-quality/

Chapter 4: Yield to Creativity

"Creativity is intelligence having fun."

- Quoted in Robinson, K. (2011). Out of Our Minds: Learning to be Creative. Capstone.

"Psychologists describe two key modes of thinking: divergent and convergent."

- Guilford, J. P. (1967). The nature of human intelligence. McGraw-Hill.

"Creative Problem Solving (CPS), pioneered by Alex Osborn and Sid Parnes."

- Osborn, A. F. (1953). Applied imagination: Principles and procedures of creative problem solving. Scribner.
- Parnes, S. J. (1967). Creative behavior guidebook. Charles Scribner's Sons.

"A 1968 study by George Land found 98% of children tested at the level of creative genius."

- Land, G., & Jarman, B. (1992). Breakpoint and beyond: Mastering the future today. HarperBusiness.

"Play lowers the stakes, fuels curiosity, and reawakens creative wiring."

- Brown, S., & Vaughan, C. (2009). Play: How it shapes the brain, opens the imagination, and invigorates the soul. Avery.

Chapter 5: Invite Connection

"Gratitude is strongly linked to greater happiness and health."

- Emmons, R. A., & McCullough, M. E. (2004). The psychology of gratitude. Oxford University Press.

"Employees who feel recognized are four times more likely to be engaged."

- Harvard Business Review. (2022, October). A better way to recognize your employees. https://hbr.org/2022/10/a-better-way-to-recognize-your-employees

"Employee recognition drives retention and boosts motivation."

- Achievers. (2022). Employee recognition statistics. https://www.achievers.com/blog/employee-recognition-statistics/
- Terryberry. (2023). Employee recognition statistics: The ultimate list. https://www.terryberry.com/blog/employee-recognition-statistics/
- Workhuman. (2023). The benefits of employee recognition. https://www.workhuman.com/blog/benefits-of-employee-recognition/

"When teams share appreciation weekly, trust deepens and connection grows."

- PlayInnové client data (internal).

Chapter 6: Normalize Reflection

"Socrates reminded us that the unexamined life is not worth living."

- Plato. (1992). Apology (G. M. A. Grube, Trans., rev. by J. Cooper). Hackett Publishing. (Original work c. 399 BCE)

"Journaling improves well-being, immune function, and memory."

- Pennebaker, J. W., & Smyth, J. M. (2016). Opening up by writing it down: How expressive writing improves health and eases emotional pain. Guilford Press.

"Organizations that pause and reflect adapt faster than those that don't."

- Harvard Business Review. (2015, April). The business case for reflection. https://hbr.org/2015/04/the-business-case-for-reflection

"Neuroscience confirms reflection consolidates learning and strengthens new neural pathways."

- Immordino-Yang, M. H., & Damasio, A. (2007). We feel, therefore we learn: The relevance of affective and social neuroscience to education. Mind, Brain, and Education, 1(1), 3–10. https://doi.org/10.1111/j.1751-228X.2007.00004.x

Chapter 7: Name Your Impact

"In the end, we are all judged by the courage of our convictions, the strength of our ideas, and the measure of our impact."

- Sandberg, S. (2013). Lean In: Women, Work, and the Will to Lead. Alfred A. Knopf.

"The Buck Stops Here."

- McCullough, D. (1992). Truman. Simon & Schuster.

"Be the change you wish to see in the world."

- Nanda, B. R. (2002). Mahatma Gandhi: A Biography. Oxford University Press.

"Any worker could pull the Andon cord."

- Liker, J. K. (2004). The Toyota Way: 14 Management Principles from the World's Greatest Manufacturer. McGraw-Hill.

"When people take ownership of outcomes... performance, collaboration, and job satisfaction all increase."

- Pierce, J. L., & Jussila, I. (2010). Collective Psychological Ownership within Organizations: Construct Introduction and Elaboration. Journal of Organizational Behavior and Human Decision Processes, 111(2), 81–93.

"Teams with clear accountability are 27% more productive..."

- Gallup. (2017). State of the American Workplace Report. Gallup, Inc.

"Leaders who model extreme ownership build trust and accelerate results."

- Cohn, J., & Moran, K. (2018). Extreme ownership in leadership. Harvard Business Review.

"Cultures of accountability directly correlate with higher retention and engagement."

- Korn Ferry. (2016). The Korn Ferry Institute Report on Leadership and Accountability. Korn Ferry International.

"Labeling emotions helps us process them."

- Willcox, G. (1982). The Feeling Wheel. Gloria Willcox.

"Naming the problem is half the battle."

- Senge, P. M. (1990). The Fifth Discipline: The Art and Practice of the Learning Organization. Doubleday.

"Companies who report transparently on ESG see higher trust and brand value."

- Eccles, R. G., Ioannou, I., & Serafeim, G. (2014). The Impact of Corporate Sustainability on Organizational Processes and Performance. Management Science, 60(11), 2835–2857.

Chapter 8: Open to All Voices

"Diversity is being invited to the party; inclusion is being asked to dance."

- Myers, V. (2016). What if I say the wrong thing? 25 habits for culturally effective people. ABA Publishing.

"Medellín transformed by listening—community councils, libraries, free transit."

- The Wall Street Journal. (2013, March 1). Medellín, Colombia named innovative city of the year. Dow Jones & Company.
- Maclean, K. (2015). Social urbanism and the politics of violence: The Medellín miracle. Palgrave Macmillan.

"IDEO's brainstorms start with silent sticky notes so no voice is lost."

- Kelley, T., & Littman, J. (2001). The art of innovation: Lessons in creativity from IDEO, America's leading design firm. Currency/ Doubleday.

"Diverse teams make better decisions 87% of the time."

- Larson, E. (2017, September 21). New research: Diversity + inclusion = better decision making at work. Forbes. https://www.forbes.com/sites/eriklarson/2017/09/21/new-research-diversity-inclusion-better-decision-making-at-work/
- Cloverpop. (2017). Hacking diversity with inclusive decision making. Cloverpop White Paper.

"Companies in the top quartile for diversity are 35% more likely to outperform financially."

- Hunt, V., Layton, D., & Prince, S. (2015). Diversity matters. McKinsey & Company.

"Inclusive teams are 80% more likely to report high performance."

- Deloitte. (2017). The diversity and inclusion revolution: Eight powerful truths. Deloitte Insights.

"Women are interrupted 33% more often than men in meetings."

- Hancock, A. B., & Rubin, B. A. (2015). Influence of communication partner's gender on language. Journal of Language and Social Psychology, 34(1), 46–64.

"Gallup found employees who feel their voice is ignored are 4.6x more likely to be disengaged."

- Gallup. (2017). State of the American Workplace Report. Gallup, Inc.

"Inclusive leadership means belonging and uniqueness drive engagement."

- Deloitte. (2016). The six signature traits of inclusive leadership. Deloitte University Press.

"Groupthink avoidance shows diverse perspectives prevent tunnel vision."

- Janis, I. L. (1982). Groupthink: Psychological studies of policy decisions and fiascoes (2nd ed.). Houghton Mifflin.

"Psychological safety allows respect and risk-taking."

- Edmondson, A. C. (2019). The fearless organization: Creating psychological safety in the workplace for learning, innovation, and growth. Wiley.

"Equity-centered design asks: who designs, who decides, who's affected?"

- Creative Reaction Lab. (2018). Equity-centered community design field guide. Creative Reaction Lab.

Chapter 9: Value is Built with Yes, And

"Neuroscientists call this the novelty effect... dopamine fires, attention sharpens, and learning accelerates."

- Lieberman, M. D. (2013). Social: Why our brains are wired to connect. Crown.

"The roots of improv trace back to 1920s Chicago... Viola Spolin developed improvisational games for children in settlement houses."

- Spolin, V. (1963). Improvisation for the theater. Northwestern University Press.

"British intelligence ran the Double-Cross System... turning enemy spies into double agents."

- Macintyre, B. (2012). Double cross: The true story of the D-Day spies. Crown.

"When 50 nations came together in San Francisco to form the United Nations... they practiced 'Yes, and' diplomacy."

- Schlesinger, S. C. (2003). Act of creation: The founding of the United Nations. Westview Press.

"When an oxygen tank exploded on Apollo 13... their improvisation turned a likely tragedy into one of history's most celebrated rescues."

- Kranz, G. (2000). Failure is not an option: Mission control from Mercury to Apollo 13 and beyond. Simon & Schuster.

"Jazz musicians in Harlem and New Orleans were practicing their own 'Yes, and.'"

- Gioia, T. (1997). The history of jazz. Oxford University Press.

"Teams using 'Yes, and' techniques generated 28% more creative ideas."

- IDEO & University of Chicago. (2001). Collaborative creativity study. (Referenced in organizational creativity literature.)

"Group creativity research shows improvisational collaboration is a strong predictor of breakthroughs."

- Sawyer, R. K. (2007). Group genius: The creative power of collaboration. Basic Books.

"Improv training as a leadership tool… leaders rated higher in adaptability and communication."

- Crossan, M. M. (1998). Improvisation in action. Organization Science, 9(5), 593–599.
- Harvard Business Review. (2018). Leadership lessons from improv. Harvard Business Publishing.

"Growth mindset shows leaders embrace challenges and evolve ideas."

- Dweck, C. S. (2006). Mindset: The new psychology of success. Random House.

Chapter 10: Advance with Play

"Play lowers stress, sparks joy, and fuels innovation."

- Brown, S., & Vaughan, C. (2009). Play: How it shapes the brain, opens the imagination, and invigorates the soul. Avery.

"3M's 15% time produced Post-it Notes."

- Hargadon, A., & Sutton, R. I. (2000). Building an innovation factory. Harvard Business Review, 78(3), 157–166.

"Google's 20% time gave birth to Gmail and Maps."

- Iyer, B. (2016, March 14). Google's famous 20% time is now

basically dead. Business Insider. https://www.businessinsider.com/
google-20-percent-time-is-dead-2015-4

"Pixar's Braintrust sessions rely on playful feedback."

- Catmull, E., & Wallace, A. (2014). Creativity, Inc.: Overcoming
the unseen forces that stand in the way of true inspiration. Random
House.

"LEGO Serious Play taps imagination through hands-on modeling."

- Kristiansen, P., & Rasmussen, R. (2014). Building a better business
using the LEGO Serious Play method. Wiley.

"When play is woven into culture, engagement and innovation rise."

- Mainemelis, C., & Ronson, S. (2006). Ideas are born in fields of play:
Towards a theory of play and creativity in organizational settings.
Research in Organizational Behavior, 27, 81–131. https://doi.
org/10.1016/S0191-3085(06)27003-5

Chapter 11: The Strategic Case for Play

"Organizations with cultures of curiosity and experimentation
outperform peers."

- Deloitte. (2019). 2019 Deloitte Human Capital Trends Report:
Leading the social enterprise. Deloitte Insights. https://www2.
deloitte.com/insights/us/en/focus/human-capital-trends/2019/
human-capital-trends.html

"Only 21% of employees worldwide feel engaged in their work."

- Gallup. (2022). State of the Global Workplace: 2022 Report. Gallup,
Inc. https://www.gallup.com/workplace/349484/state-of-the-global-
workplace-2022-report.aspx

"Humor strengthens cultures and builds resilience."

- Bitterly, T. B., Brooks, A. W., & Schweitzer, M. E. (2017). Risky
business: When humor increases and decreases status. Journal of
Personality and Social Psychology, 112(3), 431–455. https://doi.
org/10.1037/pspi0000079

"Play drives adaptability in the face of AI, hybrid work, and climate
uncertainty."

- Gratton, L. (2021). Redesigning work: How to transform your organization and make hybrid work for everyone. Penguin.

Chapter 12: Advancing Together

"The future of work isn't about flashy tech but about how teams adapt together."

- Edmondson, A. C. (2019). The fearless organization: Creating psychological safety in the workplace for learning, innovation, and growth. Wiley.

"When leaders model vulnerability, teams learn faster and innovate more."

- Coyle, D. (2018). The culture code: The secrets of highly successful groups. Bantam.

"Play gives teams a rehearsal space for pivots, adaptability, and novelty."

- Mainemelis, C., & Ronson, S. (2006). Ideas are born in fields of play: Towards a theory of play and creativity in organizational settings. Research in Organizational Behavior, 27, 81–131. https://doi.org/10.1016/S0191-3085(06)27003-5

"Teams that pause, reflect, and create in uncertainty outperform those that don't."

- Harvard Business Review. (2015, April). The business case for reflection. https://hbr.org/2015/04/the-business-case-for-reflection

"The learners will inherit the earth, while the learned find themselves equipped for a world that no longer exists."

- Hoffer, E. (1973). Reflections on the human condition. Harper & Row.

Epilogue

"Play is not the opposite of work—it's the spark that makes work human."

- Brown, S., & Vaughan, C. (2009). Play: How it shapes the brain, opens the imagination, and invigorates the soul. Avery.

"When leaders choose curiosity over certainty, cultures stay adaptive."

- Edmondson, A. C. (2019). The fearless organization: Creating psychological safety in the workplace for learning, innovation, and growth. Wiley.

"The future belongs to those who stay open, playful, and brave."

- Coyle, D. (2018). The culture code: The secrets of highly successful groups. Bantam.

www.ingramcontent.com/pod-product-compliance
Lightning Source LLC
Chambersburg PA
CBHW032100020426
42335CB00011B/426